GARDEN CITIES AND SUBURBS

Sarah Rutherford

LETCHWORTH

Ichield Way, Letchworth, in Almond Blossom Time

Where Town and Country meet

128 PAGES   PRICE SIXPENCE

Published in Great Britain in 2014 by Shire Publications Ltd,

PO Box 883, Oxford, OX1 9PL, UK.

PO Box 3985, New York, NY 10185-3985, USA.

E-mail: shire@shirebooks.co.uk   www.shirebooks.co.uk

© 2014 Sarah Rutherford.

All rights reserved. Apart from any fair dealing for the purpose of private study, research, criticism or review, as permitted under the Copyright, Designs and Patents Act, 1988, no part of this publication may be reproduced, stored in a retrieval system, or transmitted in any form or by any means, electronic, electrical, chemical, mechanical, optical, photocopying, recording or otherwise, without the prior written permission of the copyright owner. Enquiries should be addressed to the Publishers.

Every attempt has been made by the Publishers to secure the appropriate permissions for materials reproduced in this book. If there has been any oversight we will be happy to rectify the situation and a written submission should be made to the Publishers.

A CIP catalogue record for this book is available from the British Library.

Shire Library no. 782.   ISBN-13: 978 0 74781 342 2

Sarah Rutherford has asserted her right under the Copyright, Designs and Patents Act, 1988, to be identified as the author of this book.

Designed by Tony Truscott Designs, Sussex, UK and typeset in Perpetua and Gill Sans.

Cover design and photography by Peter Ashley. Back cover detail: Welgar Shredded Wheat pack showing the factory in Welwyn Garden City (author's collection).

Printed in China through Worldprint Ltd.

14 15 16 17 18   10 9 8 7 6 5 4 3 2 1

TITLE PAGE IMAGE
'Where Town and Country meet' underpinned the Garden City Movement. The publicity material promoted this key aspect of the lifestyle.

CONTENTS PAGE IMAGE
Letchworth Garden City. Typical Arts and Crafts-style housing clustered around a Parker and Unwin village green.

ACKNOWLEDGEMENTS

I would like to thank Joanna Smith, Jenifer White, Janette Ray and Jonathan Lovie for expert advice and kind encouragement. Staff at the Parker Drawing Office (home to The International Garden Cities Exhibition), Letchworth, particularly Curators Victoria Rawlings and Josh Tidy, have supplied seminal images. Members of various residents' associations have also been extremely helpful, particularly Brentham Garden Suburb, Ealing, also Westerton, Glasgow, and Silver End, Essex. Archival material has kindly been supplied by various places including East Dunbartonshire Archive, County Durham Archive, Whiteley Village, the Canadian Architectural Archive, Welwyn Garden City Heritage, and the National Archives of Australia. I would also like to thank the following people for permission to reproduce pictures as follows:

Brentham Garden Suburb Archive, pages 16 (bottom), 22, 32 (bottom), 54, 55 (bottom), 57, 72 (top); Canadian Architectural Archives, page 64; Durham County Council Peterlee Past and Present Archive (Pete0006), page 8 (bottom); East Dunbartonshire Leisure and Culture Archives, page 58; English Heritage, pages 36, 50; The Garden City Collection, title page, pages 4 (top & bottom), 6 (bottom), 8 (top), 26, 30, 31, 33, 38–41, 67 (bottom), 68 (bottom), 69–71, 72 (bottom), 73, 75 (top); The Garden Museum, pages 77, 78; Tim Green, page 13; Michael Halliwell, page 12 (bottom); John Lewis Archive, pages 45, 74 (top); Harley Jones, Rhiwbina Residents' Association, page 6 (top); King's Own Royal Regiment Museum, page 65; Jonathan Lovie, page 9; Janet Morrell, page 12 (top); National Archives of Australia (A710, 31), pages 28, 29; Janette Ray, pages 20 (top), 21, 46, 66; Unilever Archives, pages 17, 18 (top); Welwyn Garden City Heritage Centre Tony Skottowe, pages 5 (top), 74 (bottom), 75 (bottom), 76; The Whiteley Homes Trust, pages 7, 60–1, 63.

Shire Publications is supporting the Woodland Trust, the UK's leading woodland conservation charity, by funding the dedication of trees.

CONTENTS

INTRODUCTION

THIS BOOK covers garden cities, garden suburbs and garden villages. In the early twentieth century these innovative settlements provided a practical solution to decent mass housing in pleasant surroundings, often using the best designers of their day and creating popular, attractive communities. In

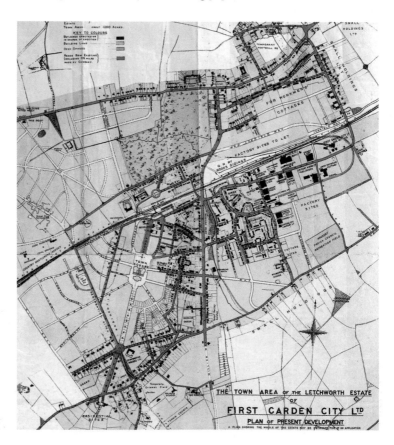

Letchworth Garden City after nine years of development, in 1912. Parker and Unwin arranged the city around Broadway, a broad spinal approach road from the south and north with the Town Square at its heart.

the early twenty-first century the ethos of the Garden City Movement on which they were founded is still felt worldwide and respected as a valid model for town planning.

These three types of settlements differed in scale. The garden city was intended by its originator, Ebenezer Howard (1850–1928), to be a large-scale, self-sustaining community laid out in zones to separate various functions. In his book of 1898 (best known under its later title of *Garden Cities of To-Morrow*), he showed how residential areas could be supported by separate areas for industry to provide employment and economic success. A civic heart included entertainment, local government and shops; there were to be public and private green spaces throughout, and all this within an agricultural setting to feed the

community. It was a huge undertaking and only three garden cities were successfully executed in Britain, at Letchworth (1903) and Welwyn (1920), in England, and Rosyth (1915) in Scotland.

The garden suburb was a smaller-scale and more easily established proposition, based on similar principles of good-quality mass housing in spacious surrounds. Crucially it was not the industrially and commercially independent unit first realised at Letchworth. Instead, the garden suburb was part of a larger conurbation, which it served, and in this it was the antithesis of Howard's self-sustaining principles. The garden suburb originated in Bedford Park, West London, begun in 1875, and with

The Shredded Wheat factory production line at Welwyn Garden City, the second English garden city.

Welwyn Garden City's 1920s neo-Georgian style set a precedent for much public housing.

Rhiwbina Garden Village, Glamorgan, waas founded in 1912 near Cardiff to a master plan by Unwin and is the best garden suburb in Wales.

nineteenth-century industrial villages such as Port Sunlight, Cheshire, and Bournville, Birmingham. While the garden suburb did not have its own factories, warehouses and civic framework, it was more than a dormitory for it usually had a strong social centre, which engendered a community spirit. Garden suburbs are found all over Britain and were embraced on the Continent and in North America, South Africa and Australia.

The interior of a house in Gidea Park designed in 1911 by Barry Parker for the Romford Garden Suburb Cottage Exhibition. The arrangement has light and airy white-painted Arts and Crafts interior.

The garden village provided another small-scale detached community, but was designed with an element of economic self-sufficiency. There were varied drivers, such as Whiteley Village, Surrey, for retired persons of small means, Jordans Village, a Quaker craft community in Bucks, and the Westfield War Memorial Village, Lancaster, built to provide employment for disabled soldiers after the First World War. Others were sustained by a factory or industry such as mining, for example Silver End, Essex (for workers at the Crittall metal window factory), the Reckitt's garden village in Hull, or the exemplary mining village at Woodlands, Doncaster.

The Garden City Movement, which promoted the philosophy of these planned settlements, quickly developed from 1898, inspired by Howard's writings. It became a broader and wider phenomenon beyond Howard and the Garden City Association, in which many of his followers developed his ideas. The Movement was embraced by a range of groups and initiatives working to control – or better plan – cities and towns that were expanding rapidly and in an unplanned way, to address the mass housing problem in a decent manner, and to improve housing conditions. Various organisations shared similar goals, such as the National Housing and Town Planning Council.

The garden city as proposed by Ebenezer Howard, and during its early years when promoted by the Garden City Association (later the Town and

At Whiteley Village, the retirement homes were all built to a very high standard following designs by seven leading Arts and Crafts architects.

Residents were proud of their garden cities. Mementoes even included crested china knick-knacks. This example is from Letchworth.

Peterlee, County Durham, was founded in 1948 under the New Towns Act of 1946. It was zoned, with the town centre ringed by housing and green spaces. It originally housed mostly coal miners and their families.

Country Planning Association), was a parallel movement with town planning, then also in its early days. As both were concerned with large-scale planning it was inevitable that their aims and principles coalesced, with the result that the clarity in the single policy of the garden city became blurred among other needs. Even so, the Movement left a hugely influential legacy. This remains dominant throughout Britain, particularly in municipal housing, and in parts of the wider world, even though Howard might not have approved of all its results.

The ideas of Howard and his followers from the 1890s were vindicated in 1946 with the passing of the New Towns Act. New Towns fulfilled many of the aims of the Garden City Movement, most comprehensively in lower housing densities within the towns, the use of green belts, employment provision, and new towns forming part of the post-war plans. This far-reaching policy was influenced by the Garden City Movement in its drive for self-sustaining and high-quality large-scale new settlements in the countryside, and affected the living standards of many whose lives it sought to improve.

THE DEVELOPMENT OF PLANNED SETTLEMENTS

Pᴸᴬᴺᴺᴇᴅ towns and villages have a long history. Many were built in Britain, from the Romans' grid-planned towns onwards. In the 1280s King Edward I ordered New Winchelsea, East Sussex to be laid out on a grid plan; Sir Christopher Wren drew up a plan (unexecuted but highly regarded) for a rationalised layout for London after the Great Fire in 1666. The New Town in Edinburgh and John Woods' buildings of Bath were architecturally exquisite examples of eighteenth-century town planning in spacious and attractive landscapes. The formal layout of streets came to be accepted as the ideal for a settlement, being economical and logical.

Estate villages proliferated in the later eighteenth and nineteenth centuries. They were built by owners who wished to relocate villages inconveniently

Milton Abbas, Dorset, built in the 1770s–80s for Lord Milton, and designed by Lancelot 'Capability' Brown. The Picturesque estate village replaced the old village in the way of Lord Milton's new park.

9

placed for their parkland proposals (Nuneham Courtenay, 1760, Milton Abbas, 1770s–80s), or who wanted a Picturesque village setting to ornament the approach to their park and mansion (Old Warden, Bedfordshire, rebuilt *c*. 1820s), or a new hamlet, redolent of an idyllic, but much idealised, rural heritage where the fashion for the Picturesque ran to extremes (Blaise Hamlet, Bristol, *c*. 1810–12, Holly Village, Highgate, 1865). Their appearance and layout was redolent of earlier, generally unplanned, villages and they were attractively built and landscaped on irregular lines, to be an ornamental feature as much as to house estate staff.

By the early nineteenth century there were many examples of planned settlements to guide the surge of demand for housing associated with the Industrial Revolution. The most socially innovative settlement was by Robert Owen (1771–1858), a self-made textile manufacturer who from 1800 to 1825 pioneered and managed a model community based on an industrial village at New Lanark, Scotland. Here he tried to achieve progress and prosperity, based on the new manufacturing techniques of the Industrial Revolution, through a caring and humane regime, reflecting Enlightenment ideals. His reforms gained New Lanark an international reputation and although it was criticised at the time, it became a model for later social reformers, particularly in areas such as infant education, working and management practices, the Co-operative Movement, trade unionism, and the Garden City Movement.

Blaise Hamlet, Bristol (*c*. 1810–12). An extreme ornamented example of a Picturesque estate village. Architect John Nash's nine different cottages surround a village green, for retired employees of Quaker banker and philanthropist John Scandrett Harford of Blaise Castle.

Owen's reforming theories were little heeded in the early to mid-nineteenth century. At this time, during the height of the Industrial Revolution, much poor-quality housing was thrown up by developers in newly expanding towns, with much exploitation of employees. However, employers gradually realised that they could maximise productivity by improving the living conditions of their workers. Robert Owen's lead gained credence. Housebuilding by large employers became common, but in utilitarian form, such as the 1840s railway towns of Swindon, Crewe and Wolverton. Developing this approach, some believed that their workforce would be still more productive and less likely to foment social unrest if they lived in better quality, controlled housing, in less cramped surroundings with access to public open space. Later in the century, living conditions were also improved by a reformed and expanding local government, driven by central government legislation, introducing measures such as by-laws controlling housing and street standards.

Notable mid-Victorian industrial villages were founded in West Yorkshire. One of the best known of these is Sir Titus Salt's Saltaire, Bradford (1850s–60s), built for workers in his textile mill. The streets of well-built terraced

Robert Owen's New Lanark, Scotland (built 1800–25). A model settlement combining both workplace and decent housing for the workers.

houses were laid out on a tightly spaced, utilitarian grid pattern, with the size and position of the houses reflecting the status of the workers in the huge adjacent factory (externally reminiscent of a great Renaissance palace), but this was set outside the town, with a large number of public benefactions including almshouses, a public park and an impressive Classical Nonconformist chapel, overshadowed by the great mill.

At the edge of Halifax Edward Akroyd commissioned designs for a

Above: Saltaire, Bradford (built 1853–63) was a model village for Titus Salt's workers at his textile mill (right), and was provided with many amenities.

more ornamental settlement from the pre-eminent Victorian architect Sir George Gilbert Scott. In Akroydon (1861–73) Akroyd housed his textile mill workers in fashionable 'Tudorbethan' style, enclosing a formal green with nearby allotments, a cemetery, and an imposing Gothic-style Anglican church. Like previous such settlements the terraced houses were built at a high density in each street, with little or nothing in the way of associated gardens. This approach became widespread and company housing was common in settlements of varying sizes and ornamentation in the later nineteenth century.

Nineteenth-century British public parks were often surrounded by spacious leafy housing developments which helped to finance the park, such as John Nash's Picturesque Regent's Park, London (1820s), Joseph Paxton's Birkenhead Park (1847, one of the earliest public parks), and numerous others. But these did not directly influence town planning, coming more as a welcome incident for wealthy residents.

Akroydon was built by Edward Akroyd in 1861–73 at the edge of Halifax for his workers, with good-quality housing and communal amenities including a park.

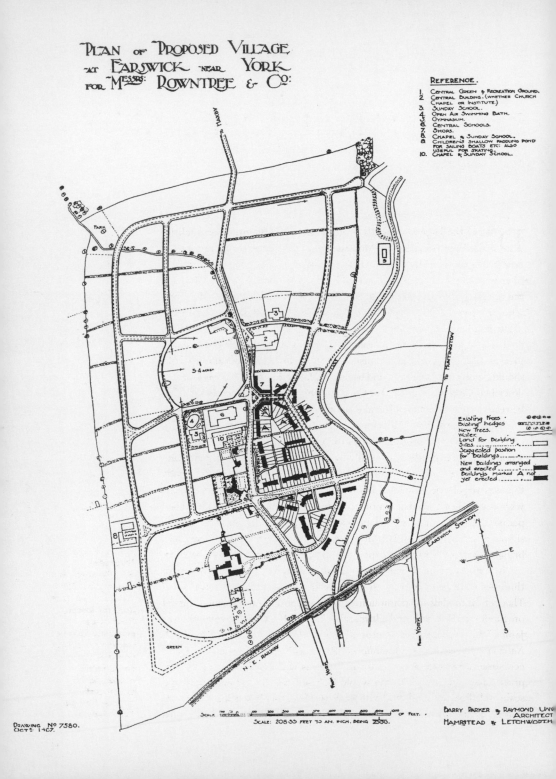

PLAN OF PROPOSED VILLAGE
AT EARSWICK NEAR YORK
FOR MESSRS. ROWNTREE & CO.

REFERENCE.

1. CENTRAL GREEN & RECREATION GROUND.
2. CENTRAL BUILDING. (WHETHER CHURCH CHAPEL OR INSTITUTE.)
3. SUNDAY SCHOOL.
4. OPEN AIR SWIMMING BATH.
5. GYMNASIUM.
6. CENTRAL SCHOOLS.
7. SHOPS.
8. CHAPEL & SUNDAY SCHOOL.
9. CHILDREN'S SHALLOW PADDLING POND FOR SAILING BOATS ETC: ALSO USEFUL FOR SKATING.
10. CHAPEL & SUNDAY SCHOOL.

Existing Trees.
Existing hedges.
New Trees.
Water.
Land for Building Sites.
Suggested position for buildings.
New buildings arranged and erected.
Buildings marked A not yet erected.

DRAWING Nº 7580.
OCTº 1907.

SCALE 208.33 FEET TO AN INCH. BEING 2500.

BARRY PARKER & RAYMOND UNWIN
ARCHITECT
HAMPSTEAD & LETCHWORTH

INFLUENTIAL IDEAS AND EXAMPLES

D URING the later nineteenth century various influential personalities shaped the Garden City Movement in the immediate run-up to the creation of the first garden city. Underpinning its philosophy were the ideas of writers such as Augustus Pugin (1812–52), John Ruskin (1819–1900) and the towering Arts and Crafts and Socialist figure William Morris (1834–96) who promoted universal dignity of labour, improved design and 'decency of surroundings'. Morris described a Utopian rural way of life in his visionary Socialist novel *News From Nowhere* (1890) in which all work is creative and pleasurable, based on the premise that 'the material surroundings of life should be pleasant, generous, and beautiful'. In 1891 a review in *The Guardian* described his book as an 'idyll of Communism ... beautiful but perverse,' to be read 'as poetry not as political economy'.

The Arts and Crafts Movement is now best known for its aesthetic of craftsmanship expressed in traditional styles, but this was only part of a whole lifestyle expressed practically by architects, planners, designers, and craftsmen on a small scale during the later nineteenth century. Ironically this was largely via individual houses for middle- and upper-class patrons who could afford what was not economically available to working-class people. Morris's ideas mixed political reform with a romantic artistic simplicity, which fitted well with the ideals of the Garden City Movement, bringing Arts and Crafts concepts and a pleasurable lifestyle to the masses.

In the nineteenth century much consideration was given by progressive thinkers to urban planning to improve living conditions for workers. Theoretical models for communities were proposed. An influential model on Ebenezer Howard, and ultimately the Garden City Movement, was James Silk Buckingham's 'Victoria', described and depicted in his book *National Evils and Practical Remedies* (1849). Buckingham included social and economic aspects to make the town viable, as well as to make it physically practical and pleasing. Victoria would be a self-contained town on a large scale, self-financed and run with each resident owning at least one £20 share. The town was zoned concentrically into various areas of use, with

Opposite: New Earswick was designed in 1902 on the outskirts of York for Joseph Rowntree's chocolate-factory workers. This was planners Parker and Unwin's prototype for Letchworth Garden City the following year.

Buckingham's model town of Victoria shows an early concept of concentric zoning, which influenced Ebenezer Howard's garden city model (*National Evils and Practical Remedies*, 1849).

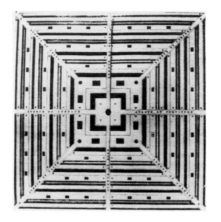

Bedford Park, west London (1875 onwards), was one of the first coherent Arts and Crafts suburbs and was highly influential on planned settlements.

an expansive ornamented landscape, and a surrounding agricultural belt to supply food.

Executed on a smaller scale, Bedford Park in west London was one of the first coherent Arts and Crafts housing developments. It formed a complete, if compact, suburb whose harmonious architecture was set in gardens in spacious streets, in concept following on from the spacious developments built to help finance public parks. It was developed privately over several decades from 1875, with stately Queen Anne-style houses mainly by the great architects Richard Norman Shaw (1831–1912) and Philip Webb (1831–1915). Around 350 houses were built, the estate incorporating extant trees, and providing community facilities. It is regarded as the world's first garden suburb, a

SUNLIGHT SOAP

PORT SUNLIGHT
VIEW OF WORKS
& Houses for Employés.
AREA OF SITE, 114 ACRES.
& OF WORKS, WHARF & SIDING
29 ACRES
Capacity 2400 Tons of Soap
per week.

WORKS & VILLAGE, PORT SUNLIGHT.

model that was emulated not just by the Garden City Movement, but by suburban developments worldwide. Sir John Betjeman described Bedford Park as 'the most significant suburb built in the last [nineteenth] century, probably in the western world'.

Alongside the genteel Bedford Park two late nineteenth-century industrial villages epitomised the social and economic benefits of attractive housing for workers in a landscaped setting in Picturesque style. William Hesketh Lever (1851–1925), later Lord Leverhulme, built Port Sunlight for his adjacent palm oil soapworks in the Wirral. The Cadbury family's Bournville village served the recently relocated chocolate factory on the outskirts of Birmingham. Port Sunlight is the more important architecturally but Bournville is the more significant socially.

Although Port Sunlight and Bournville reflected the values of Robert Owen and his followers, together with developments like Saltaire and Akroydon they showed other influences and innovations. House plans were improved, becoming more convenient and spacious. Houses occupied a largely irregular layout, their arrangement embracing a proportion of detached and semi-detached as well as short terraces, developing the Picturesque heritage by using the English vernacular in a suburban context. Most innovatively these villages were designed to be full of gardens and greenery: large hedged gardens, public open spaces and spacious tree- and

Port Sunlight, Cheshire, in 1900 before its layout was completed by Thomas Mawson. This industrial village was built to the highest standards by Lord Leverhulme from the 1880s, for workers at his adjacent palm oil soapworks in the Wirral.

17

Vernacular styles proliferated in highly ornamented fashion at Port Sunlight, including fine imitations of the local Cheshire timber-frame tradition, such as the Post Office.

Port Sunlight was one of the first industrial villages to depart from a grid pattern layout and to emphasise the amenity setting of the houses. Thomas Mawson's development plan (1914) used formal Beaux-Arts-style boulevards to unite the design, in a similar manner to Letchworth.

grass-verge-lined streets and boulevards, responding to existing features and retaining mature trees and woodland wherever possible.

At Port Sunlight from 1888 Lever executed his architectural dream in a philanthropic new village. He employed many notable architects to create an exceptionally attractive, Picturesque layout, with tree-lined streets, open

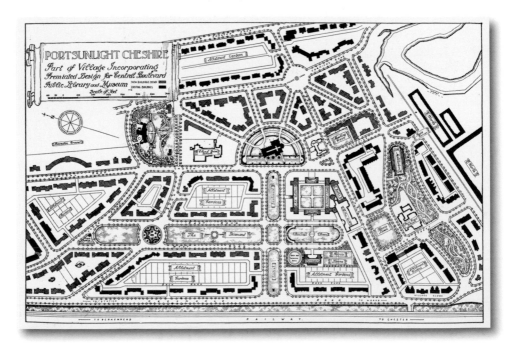

spaces and parks, and imposing formal spaces and buildings at the civic heart. The houses, initially in local vernacular village styles dubbed collectively as 'Old English', were grouped in broad streets with open frontages and back yards, with communal allotments behind. Even the Post Office was a fine example of the local Cheshire timber framing style. Houses were relatively spacious, each with a kitchen, scullery, parlour and three or four bedrooms.

Port Sunlight attracted much comment and was widely and approvingly publicised. In his seminal 1904 book *Das Englische Haus* (*The English House*), the German Anglophile Hermann Muthesius wrote, 'Port Sunlight will always be honoured by the highest recognition.' In the handbook to the 1910 International Town Planning Conference, Patrick Abercrombie wrote of Port Sunlight that it was 'one of the earliest of the self-contained "garden villages", which has exercised an enormous amount of influence on English and foreign planning.' Its key drawback as a model for the wider world was that it was never intended to be a self-sufficient commercial proposition and was heavily subsidised by the company.

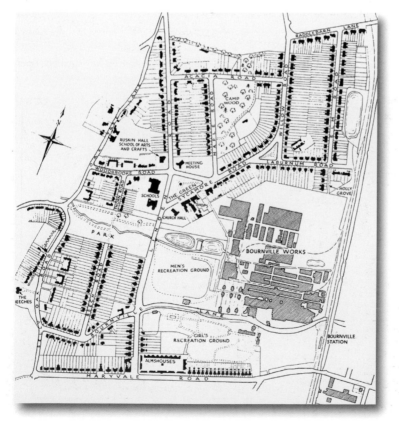

George Cadbury's Bournville, begun in 1895, was not restricted to his factory workers. As at Port Sunlight, the large factory dominated the settlement and the green spaces around the houses were important.

Hallway and stairs of a cottage at Bournville (1906). The layout was designed to be practical and efficient, making the most of the space available.

The houses at Bournville were less self-consciously ornamental and more cost-effective than at Port Sunlight, while providing a good standard of housing with large gardens and much open space.

Still more influential on the Garden City Movement was Quaker George Cadbury's (1839–1922) Bournville, begun in 1895 on 120 acres of land. It was always a more realistic commercial proposition than Port Sunlight, less ostentatious in its civic provision and buildings, so that commercial rents would eventually cover the costs. The delicate balance of affordable and attractive living standards (and the religious connection) soon led Bournville to become a model for another Quaker chocolate manufacturer's industrial village, Joseph Rowntree's New Earswick, York. This, in turn, was the practical proving ground for the architects and planners Raymond Unwin and Barry Parker, immediately before the embarked on laying out the first garden city, Letchworth, in 1903.

The ornamental layout of Bournville, like Port Sunlight, had both formal and informal lines and open spaces and parks, but it was less self-consciously

Picturesque and grew in phases without an overall development plan. The initial layout was drawn up by the Quaker surveyor A. P. Walker in 1894, responding to various existing features including roads, woodland and mature trees. The provision of private and public open spaces and their arrangement was as important as the buildings. Gardens were extremely important for produce and their carefully considered size was intended to be enough for a worker to manage alongside his main job, reducing his outgoings. The Cadburys had a great influence on the way of life especially via the range of amenities, the cottages and their layout and gardens. Various educational and religious institutions were built around a large green, and shops and recreational facilities were provided. To give the residents more control, the Tenants' Village Council was founded 'to promote the Social, Educational, and Recreative life of the village'. It was an industrial village with industrial decentralisation, which became the central tenet of the garden city ideal.

Bournville was an experiment in housing reform. It was intended to have a wide audience as a financially realistic solution to decent housing for the masses. Unlike conventional industrialists' settlements it was not built exclusively for Cadbury's own employees but was handed over to an independent body, the Bournville Village Trust, in 1900. Like Port Sunlight, it was much publicised via contributions to conferences, articles, and handbooks such as Harvey's *The Model Village and its Cottages: Bournville* (1906), and *Typical Plans* [of] *the Bournville Village Trust* (1911).

The 1901 Garden City Association Conference was held by invitation at Bournville, promoting the Garden City Movement, which attracted three hundred delegates (the 1902 conference at Port Sunlight attracted one thousand). This was a gathering of many who became influential in the planning world, including key personalities such as Muthesius, the landscape designer and planner Thomas Mawson, and Patrick Geddes. At Bournville, Howard observed in 1906, 'A garden village has been built, a garden city is but a step beyond'. Bournville inspired other developments, but as pioneering and egalitarian settlements rather than industrialists' villages run on paternalistic lines. These included the nearby Moor Pool, Harborne (1907–12), founded as an egalitarian co-partnership scheme.

Plan of living areas from *The Model Village and its Cottages: Bournville* (1906, Alexander Harvey). The living spaces were carefully planned for comfort, efficiency and hygiene. Harvey was one of the main designers of the cottages at Bournville.

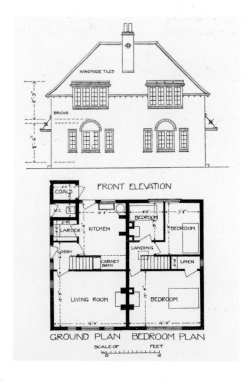

FRONT ELEVATION

GROUND PLAN BEDROOM PLAN

CO-PARTNERSHIP MANAGEMENT SCHEMES

Co-partnership management schemes were at the heart of many of these developments and gave residents greater equality and influence in their running. They were intended to ensure both commercial and social solidarity arising from the bonds of common interest. Tenants were made joint owners, with outside financiers or developers, of the houses they occupied, with the estate managed by an elected committee of shareholders. Further land could be purchased and all houses would be held in common, the absence of private individual ownership reinforcing each tenant's personal interest in the prosperity of the development as a whole. Co-partnerships were a fundamental tenet of many such schemes in the early twentieth century before local authority housing became widespread. The earliest included those at Brentham, Ealing (a suburb, begun 1901), Letchworth Garden City (1903), Humberstone, Leicester (a suburb, begun 1906) and Hampstead Garden Suburb (founded 1905). Further schemes were founded after the First World War, sometimes as Public Utility Societies such as Onslow Garden Village, Guildford (1920) and from 1936 as Housing Associations.

Advertisement for the first co-partnership housing scheme, at Brentham, Ealing, the home of this more egalitarian ownership system.

New Earswick was founded by Quaker chocolate manufacturer Joseph Rowntree (1836–1925), having been inspired by the 1901 Garden City Association Conference at Bournville. Rowntree was impressed at Bournville and met the young and idealistic architect and planner Raymond Unwin. Cadbury advised Rowntree on this development. The New Earswick Trust was based closely on the Trust Deed and objectives of Bournville Village Trust, and it became a testing ground for garden city design standards. It was to be a balanced settlement where houses were available to anyone, not just employees of Rowntree. As at Bournville, a combination of economy with art was required. Even so, Parker and Unwin drew on the traditions of village design tailored to the unique characteristics of the site itself to provide as much individuality as possible. Both villages were influential as exemplary schemes combining visual appeal and good living conditions as well as economical viability, but New Earswick was physically distanced from the factory, unlike Port Sunlight and Bournville where the factory dominated. Other Nonconformist industrialists' villages based on similar planned lines included Reckitts' Hull Garden Village and Colmans at Norwich. Woodlands near Doncaster, designed in 1907, applied this kind of layout to the most innovative mining village of the time.

All this pointed towards how Utopia could be achieved in practice. Some believed Bournville was the realisation of William Morris's Utopia. The radical critic George Haw was dewy-eyed: 'At every turn in the lanes and tree-planted streets I was reminded of William Morris' picture in *News from Nowhere*.' Even so the adjacent factory was ever present.

Influential town planning movements and architectural styles developed in Europe and North America. In Germany municipally prepared plans were adopted for the long-term development of suburban areas. The term 'garden city' had been coined in America well before 1890. The Beaux-Arts style, influential in town planning in the later nineteenth century, became popular in Continental Europe and the United States. It was an architectural style originating in France characterised by classical forms, symmetry, rich ornamentation, and a grand scale. The style was epitomised in town planning by the grand layout of Hausmann's Paris, where, for the first time, parks and green spaces were integrated into the design.

The 1893 World's Fair in Chicago celebrated on an extensive scale the discovery of America. It was an inventive and hugely popular exhibition whose innovative spacious and zoned plan owed much to the great American landscape architect Frederick Law Olmsted. Olmsted had also in 1869 planned the nearby town, Riverside, one of the first planned suburban communities

Many New Earswick houses were relatively plain but the quality of living was important, with large gardens, much communal space and many amenities.

in the United States, in which 700 of its 16,000 acres were occupied by green roads, borders, parks and other features, blending town and country. The layout offered an alternative to the grid plans and high-density housing in New York and Chicago. The exhibition inspired Daniel Burnham to design a plan in 1895 for improving Chicago, which he called the City Beautiful – itself the expression of a movement that tried to bring order, system and pattern to chaotic urban growth in the United States.

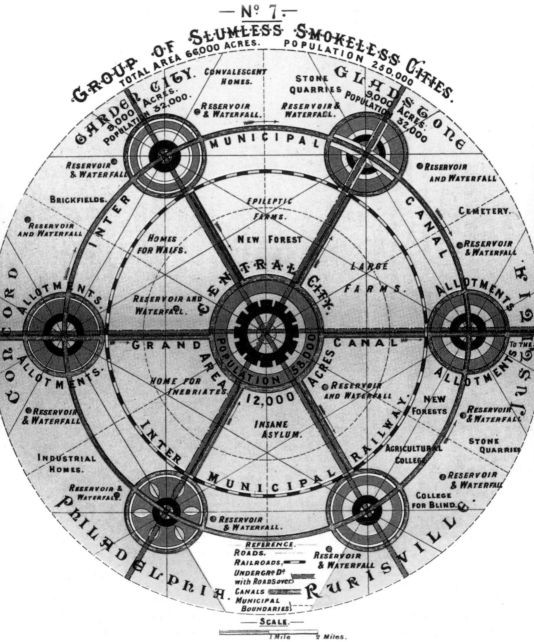

HOWARD, PARKER AND UNWIN: GARDEN CITY THEORY AND PLANNING

B Y THE 1890s these political, social and economic theories had matured and planned settlements proliferated as models to a point that allowed their combined expression in practice. Initially a theoretical approach was codified by social reformer Ebenezer Howard (1850–1928) in his book *Tomorrow: A Peaceful Path to Real Reform* (1898), which was so popular that it was soon reissued as *Garden Cities of Tomorrow* (1902). He was the catalyst who drew together many like-minded theories and people, in a scheme combining a sense of community and coherent planning structure. Howard, a shorthand reporter, had spent several years in Chicago in the 1870s, and was widely read and socially idealistic. He would have known of Olmsted's Riverside, and perhaps visited. His ideas on the provision of good-quality housing in pleasant, healthy surroundings for a social mix of residents were enthusiastically received as viable by those who were sympathetic and in a position to promote them and ensure that they were translated into action. The basis of his theory was that town and country should be united in his term 'garden cities', to enjoy the best of both, with low-density housing, green belts and defined residential, amenity and industrial zones.

Howard's book mainly addressed the processes to make the garden city work as a self-sufficient city with a social purpose. This was based on a sound financial foundation, and administration via an elected Central Council. He defined 'garden city' as a city in a garden (i.e. surrounded by countryside), not a city of gardens, although this latter concept was applied, with his approval, by the planners who executed his ideas. He never regarded the book as '... more than a sketch or outline of what we hoped to accomplish.' Only a fraction covers the layout, which he acknowledged should be designed by specialists. Instead, he illustrated a notional schema in diagrams.

The City was divided into zones for various activities, ensuring industry and residential areas were separated, with a civic centre and public gardens. This was influenced by Buckingham's Victoria, but it also reflected wider social concerns and proposed solutions. Howard passionately believed that a low-density settlement would bring together the benefits of both town

Opposite: Howard's model united the best aspects of the town and country. The central compact population (58,000) in the town of Garden City was linked by canals, railways and roads to further compact satellite settlements through the surrounding agricultural land. From *Tomorrow: A Peaceful Path to Real Reform* (1898).

Ebenezer Howard
(1850–1928),
father of the
Garden City
Movement
(Spencer Pryse,
1912).

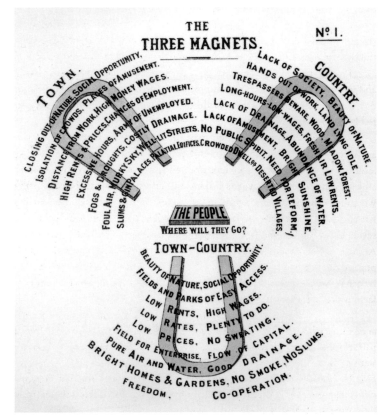

Howard's 'Three
Magnets' diagram
brilliantly
summarised his
'joyous union' of
town and country,
which he believed
was the best
solution to the
housing question.
From *Tomorrow:*
A Peaceful Path
to Real Reform
(1898).

and country in the 'garden city'. Such a settlement, as a vehicle of social reform, with social mixing and where tenants became part owners (for example in co-partnerships), would provide a productive life in healthy and pleasant surroundings, free from exploitation, echoing Morris's romanticised rural lifestyle in *News from Nowhere* (1890).

Howard's true garden city was a civic entity, sustainable and self-contained in provision for its residents who were to have a financial stake in their homes. It would occupy a virgin site unrelated to other settlements, certainly not extending the sprawling reach of an existing town or city. However, only two true garden cities were built in England: Letchworth Garden City (founded in 1903) and Welwyn Garden City (founded in 1920), although the theories greatly influenced town planning throughout the century.

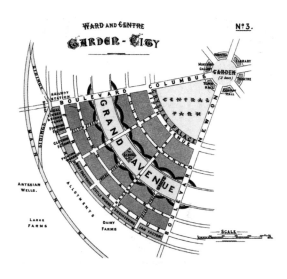

Howard's concentric land-use zoning separated residential and amenity areas from industry and transport, with wide boulevards linking them to the civic heart. From *Tomorrow: A Peaceful Path to Real Reform* (1898).

Howard defined a garden city as: ' ... a town designed for healthy living and industry; of a size that makes possible a full measure of social life, but not larger; surrounded by a rural belt; the whole of the land being in public ownership or held in trust for the community.'

His scheme was based on an extensive rural canvas, detached from any other conurbation, with a green belt separating the cities, containing allotments, smallholdings, agricultural land, woodland, recreational areas and railways, canals and roads linking the cities. The agricultural setting would form an efficient and reliable local supply of food for the city, allowing fair agricultural rewards for farmers and smallholders. This would form the setting for a central city of 58,000 population occupying a 12,000 acre site. Around this he proposed a cluster of six detached satellite cities of 32,000 population covering 6,000 acres in 1,000 acres of urban development divided by farm land. The population would be socially mixed, with a range of facilities for a full social life.

Land-use zoning was a key feature of his scheme. A central group of civic and community buildings surrounded a large garden with a covered 'crystal palace' for shopping and a large park. This in turn was surrounded by housing with gardens crossed by avenues and boulevards, including a 3 mile-long circular boulevard. The outermost zone of development was for industry with a narrow ring of factories at the periphery, separated from the housing by a green belt, and encircled by a railway.

Zoning within the city was a key part of Eliel Saarinen's unexecuted plan for Australia's new capital, Canberra (1911): blue for open spaces, black blocks for 'important buildings', purple blocks around red for flats and shops, brown for individual houses.

Howard saw the practical benefit of a pilot scheme: 'One small Garden City must be built as a working model, and then a group of cities …'. Less realistically he hoped that with such a shining example 'the reconstruction of London must inevitably follow'.

The model caught the imagination of influential reformers. In 1899 the Garden City Association was founded. It proposed to build the first garden city, and rapidly raised £156,000 to buy land in Hertfordshire and initiate the project.

Naturally many members and followers of the Garden City Association believed strongly in Morris's ideals, and were Socialists and members of the Fabian Society (which believed in social reform by peaceful and gradual means). The appeal of the garden city was that it served a whole range of social groups. One of the most influential advocates was Howard's disciple and spiritual successor (Sir) Frederic Osborn (1885–1978), who became the foremost town planner of the mid-twentieth century. Having been a housing official at Letchworth, he assisted Howard to set up Welwyn Garden City in the 1920s, and then applied garden city theories to town planning. He transformed the Garden City Association into the influential Town and Country Planning Association and greatly contributed to shaping the New Towns Act of 1946, which led to over thirty New Towns being built in Britain.

Many progressive thinkers were so committed to the idea that they invested in the garden cities, including Howard's friend George Bernard Shaw, who nicknamed him 'Ebenezer the Garden City Geyser', for his continual 'spouting forth' on the advantages of garden city living.

Many progressive middle-class women were drawn to the Movement, but few women were directly influential. Exceptions included Henrietta Barnett, who founded Hampstead Garden Suburb in 1905, architect Ethel Charles, who designed cottages at Letchworth around 1905, and Mary Higgs, who with Sarah Lees promoted Oldham Garden Suburb from 1907. Architect Elizabeth Scott had her first post as an architectural assistant at Welwyn before creating her prize-winning design in 1928 for the Stratford Shakespeare Memorial Theatre.

Satellite settlements linked to a central core were integral to W. B. Griffin's 1911 winning design for Canberra, reminiscent of Howard's theories.

Right: Barry Parker (1867–1947). After the partnership with Unwin dissolved in 1914 he continued his successful town planning practice.

Far right: Raymond Unwin (1863–1940). After partnership with Parker, and advising on many garden suburbs, he moved into public sector work and promoted garden city principles, influencing public sector housing standards and models between the wars.

Architects and planners Barry Parker (1867–1947) and Raymond Unwin (1863–1940) were the like-minded specialists ideally suited to pioneer Howard's theories and translate them into practice as a real scheme. Not only did they do this but they embraced the whole concept enthusiastically, applied it to many further schemes and fervently spread the word. As such their careers became integral to the Garden City Movement (c. 1900–30). They also ensured its continued influence on mass housing and town planning, not least as Unwin became the most influential early-twentieth-century town planner, and the garden city concept became arguably the most influential export of British Town Planning. Parker and Unwin avoided flats as were commonly used in Europe. Instead, based on the Englishman's love for his house and garden, they used this unit at low density as the basis for their work, including for the first garden city.

The two men were closely related (including as brothers-in-law) and like-minded, being interested in social issues and reform, and enthusiasts for the views of Morris and Ruskin. In 1896 they set up an architectural practice together. They embraced the Arts and Crafts Movement, favoured simple vernacular styles and 'cottage' furnishings, and aimed to improve housing standards for the working classes. Within the partnership Unwin generally devised the strategy and layout, and Parker the aesthetic detail. Early on, Unwin was particularly concerned with the grouping of buildings, especially the idea of the village green and the arrangement of houses around it, as a small cohesive community drawing on historic precedent. This particularly influenced the garden cities and early garden suburbs.

The commissions of their partnership chart key milestones in the Garden City Movement, which in turn influenced much public housing development throughout the twentieth century. Between 1903 and 1914, Parker and Unwin undertook many of the most influential projects to

Parker and Unwin's Letchworth Office oozed the Arts and Crafts principles of craftsmanship of an earlier vernacular age.

The Letchworth office exterior resembled a romanticised East Anglian thatched medieval hall house in a spacious garden adjacent to the public park. It was enlarged and is now the home of the Parker Drawing Office (home to The International Garden Cities Exhibition).

develop settlements based on garden city principles. Unwin in particular designed or advised on many garden suburb master plans in England, Scotland and Wales, including Brentham, Glasgow (Westerton) and Rhiwbina, Cardiff. They also were at the heart of a group of like-minded planners and architects who shared a kind of camaraderie and disseminated the ethos of decent housing in attractive and healthy surroundings.

Unwin's self-contained village green surrounded by houses was a hallmark of the Garden City Movement (*Town Planning in Practice: An Introduction to the Art of Designing Cities and Suburbs*, 1909).

Brentham, Ealing was a typical garden suburb layout by Parker and Unwin (1907); note the irregular street patterns where houses enclosed communal open spaces for lawns or hedged allotments.

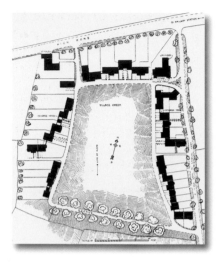

To start with, though, in 1902 they were invited to design New Earswick, York, for Rowntree, heavily influenced by Bournville. New Earswick was their proving ground for Letchworth Garden City when, in 1903, the First Garden City Company adopted their plan and so began their long relationship with the first garden city. Here they based their office. Letchworth provided an unrivalled opportunity to show (and publicise) how a true garden city could be planned to work practically as a self-sufficient civic unit in attractive, socially mixed surroundings that engendered true community spirit. Although not all their proposals were implemented, and commercial imperatives sometimes

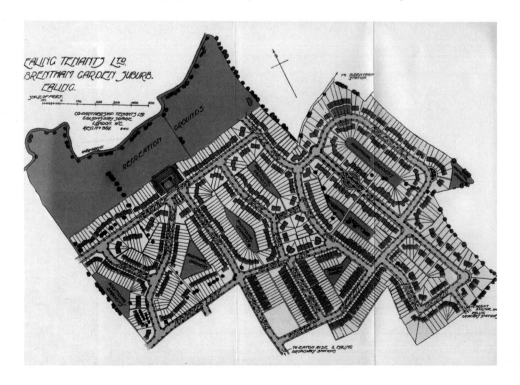

diluted the original concept, their vision pioneered and epitomised the ideals of the Movement in practice and proved that they were, to a great extent, realistic.

Letchworth was a huge job, but the practice continued to work on other similar major projects and fostered a number of like-minded architects and planners. In 1905 Henrietta Barnett commissioned them to plan the Garden Suburb at Hampstead, in association with the fashionable architect Edwin Lutyens (not a meeting of minds). In 1906 Unwin left Letchworth for Hampstead. Parker continued the supervision role in Letchworth as well as the design of some 275 dwellings and a number of

Westholme, Letchworth, reflects Unwin's village green sketch, with irregular frontages to the road and large back gardens.

Below: At junctions houses were set back by Unwin in a variety of ways to avoid dominating the street scene (1909).

public buildings. In 1907 Ealing Tenants Limited, the first co-partnership, appointed Parker and Unwin to plan the development of the second phase of Brentham garden suburb in west London. This was typical of their layouts for garden suburbs. Unwin took on many other commissions for garden suburbs and co-partnership housing throughout Britain, whose development often stalled at the outbreak of the First World War. Many of their techniques were set out and illustrated in Unwin's influential book *Town Planning in Practice: An Introduction to the Art of Designing Cities and Suburbs* (1909), which combined images and theories on urban design.

In 1914 the two dissolved the partnership to pursue their particular interests. Parker continued his town planning practice, advising on Porto, Portugal in 1915 and São Paulo, Brazil in 1917–19. From 1927 to 1941 he advised Manchester City Council on developing the model Manchester suburb of Wythenshawe. Although it was intended as a third garden city, it remained in reality a suburb with an industrial zone, although praised by Unwin in 1945 as 'the most perfect example of a garden city'.

Unwin moved into public sector work and promoted garden city principles in government during the First World War, having joined the Local Government Board in December 1914. He applied the principles devised for earlier commissions to build homes rapidly and economically, including satisfactory standards for gardens, family privacy and internal spaces. In 1915 for the Ministry of Munitions he designed the villages of Gretna and Eastriggs and supervised others. From 1917 he had a deeply influential role at the Tudor Walters Committee on working-class housing, whose report was published in 1918 and influenced much inter-war public housing. This report broke from Howard's key concept, proposing that the new developments should be satellites of existing towns rather than completely separate garden cities. Unwin and Parker had determined that the minimum standard for housing density was nine houses per acre, a standard that was adopted in the 1919 Housing Act and used for private and municipal estates in England. In 1919 Unwin became Chief Architect to the newly formed Ministry of Health, and was Chief Technical Officer for Housing and Town Planning when he retired in 1928. As technical adviser to the Greater London Regional Planning Committee he largely wrote its two major reports (1929 and 1933). He was the driving force behind the type of inter-war municipal housing so common today.

GARDEN CITIES IN PRACTICE

THE FIRST garden city was built on the Letchworth Hall estate, near Hitchin, Hertfordshire. It was founded as an industrial town in 1903 on funds raised by the well-connected Liberal MP, Ralph Neville QC, who at Howard's invitation had become the dynamic first President of the Garden City Association in 1899. The investment did not offer a very secure proposition to the average investor, but enough influential men of means with an interest in the scheme and more than ordinary nerve and resolution were willing to invest, and in the first year over £100,000 was raised. The land was acquired in 1903 by the Garden City Pioneer Company Limited (which became the First Garden City Limited and included Howard and Neville on its board), together with other agricultural land, in total nearly 4,000 acres. By 1910 there were 2,300 shareholders, 6,500 residents and 1,300 houses and other buildings. By 1914 the population had risen to 14,500.

Parker and Unwin's winning layout plan arranged the City around Broadway, a broad, avenue-lined spinal approach road from the south and north (originally intended for tramway provision which was never carried out). Broadway opened into a formal central square, around which it was intended to range the main religious and civic buildings. These in turn were to be flanked by a geometrical layout of shops and residential development reached along broad, tree-lined boulevards radiating through residential areas out to the factories. A group of grand civic buildings was to surround the square, but this never materialised. Instead the open space was surrounded by Lombardy poplars, planted in 1914 to indicate the outline of the planned buildings, and it was gradually enclosed piecemeal by civic and other public buildings. Crucial industry was sited in its own zone separated from housing and the civic centre.

Naturally, the first garden city did not slavishly follow Howard's theoretical model, but it reflected many of the main principles including:

- The best aspects of town and country integrated in a controlled way.
- Zoned land use: housing, public open space and industry within an agricultural setting forming a 'green belt'.

Opposite: Welwyn Garden City, the second garden city, designed in 1920 by Louis de Soissons. The great formal double boulevard, Parkway, leads to the campus, echoing the centred layout of the first garden city.

- A central civic nucleus of institutions, and a shopping centre with a formal civic space.
- Low-density housing (maximum twelve per acre), even for industrial workers.
- Broad, tree-lined streets and boulevards throughout.

Satellite settlements were not proposed in the surrounding countryside, but distinct residential communities formed part of the whole, each with its own church, with Unwin's attached perimeter villages or suburbs on the scale of New Earswick. Even so the mixing of social classes was still not achieved.

In planning the layout Parker and Unwin incorporated existing natural features, but they were not afraid of using formality to unite the city at its heart. Unwin had explained their approach at the first Garden City Association Conference in 1901:

The combined benefits of town and country living enticed new residents to Letchworth.

HEALTH of the COUNTRY COMFORTS of the TOWN

LETCHWORTH
The FIRST GARDEN CITY

The successful setting out of such a work as a new city will only be accomplished by the frank acceptance of the natural conditions of the site; and, humbly bowing to these, by the fearless following out of some definite and orderly design based on them … such natural features should be taken as the note of the composition; but beyond this there must be no meandering in a false imitation of so-called natural lines.

Parker and Unwin designed much of the housing as well as the town plan around a Beaux-Arts-style formal axial road network focused on Broadway. The area close to Broadway was the most prestigious with lowest-density houses, many detached, and spacious gardens; the outer areas close to the industrial area were developed with a significant amount of higher-density artisans' housing, although low-density houses around several 'village greens' were also laid out. A public park, Howard Park and Garden, was placed (1904–11) in a residential area close to the civic centre, but its serpentine lines contrasted with the formality of Broadway.

HOWARD MEMORIAL HALL.   GARDEN CIT

Here the Mrs Howard Memorial Hall (Parker and Unwin, 1905–6), the first public building in the Garden City, was built, not surprisingly in Arts and Crafts style. It was named after Howard's first wife, Lizzie, who had died in 1904 having patiently helped and encouraged him to spread the gospel of the garden city. It housed the first Council meetings.

The architecture was rooted in Arts and Crafts principles, with attractive styles based on vernacular precedents and a studied avoidance of obvious regularity. This was the hallmark of the early garden suburbs up to 1914. Certain materials were favoured, with characteristic pebbledash or painted roughcast brick walls and tiled roofs. Slate and the local yellow brick were avoided as unattractive, but red brick was used for civic buildings and larger houses, giving them gravitas. Several imposing civic buildings were erected at the heart of Broadway in what was considered an appropriately formal Queen Anne style, leavened by Arts and Crafts touches. Rather quaintly Parker and Unwin's own offices were built in 1906–7 in the form of an East Anglian thatched medieval hall house, with roughcast walls and surrounded by a romantic garden. The whole was redolent of romantic, William Morris-inspired idealism.

Practically, it proved difficult to ensure that the housing styles presented a visual quality and unity throughout the town. Although eminent architects designed some houses, these stood alongside speculative builders' designs. Initially it was difficult to attract industry because of the lack of working-class housing. To help offset this the company ran the 1905 Cheap Cottages Exhibition, a competition that attracted eminent socially-minded architects to design housing for poorer families at reasonable cost, up to £150. With nationwide press coverage the exhibition attracted over 60,000 visitors to

The Mrs Howard Memorial Hall, Howard Park, Letchworth (Parker and Unwin, 1905–6) in Arts and Crafts style. It served the community in memory of Ebenezer Howard's first wife and helpmeet.

The Nook Cottage, by architect George E. Clare, was one of the most popular 1905 Exhibition Cottages. One report said: 'I think the best arranged and the prettiest of all the buildings was "The Nook Cottage", a marvel of cheapness at £150. The rooms are all on the ground floor, and the kitchen, with its recessed inglenook round the big fireplace, and its box seats to economise space, are reminiscent of the rural homes one finds in real, old-fashioned garden cities, the villages and hamlets of Old England.'

the Garden City so that it became a household name. Over 130 houses were built, including innovative designs such as one of the world's first prefabricated concrete buildings (158 Wilbury Road), in which expensive timber was replaced by poured concrete wherever possible. The plethora of styles, while fulfilling the social and aesthetic ideal of Morris and the Arts and Crafts Movement, did little for visual unity.

The most eminent architect to contribute at Letchworth was M. H. Baillie Scott (1865–1945). Although he designed only a few houses, they were particularly influential. His pair of semi-detached houses, Elmwood Cottages, for the 1905 Exhibition was not only compact and economical to build, but artistic in appearance. Other architects made high-quality contributions, including several of Parker and Unwin's former assistants. Of these, C. M. Crickmer (1879–1971) was one of the most important and prolific garden city architects and the most important Letchworth architect after Parker

A first-prize-winning cottage at Letchworth Garden City. It was compact but well designed with a living room, three bedrooms and a 'working kitchen'.

and Unwin. Crickmer also worked on buildings for Hampstead Garden Suburb (1906 onwards), Welwyn Garden City (1920 onwards), and the 1911 Gidea Park Competition. Ethel Charles (1871–1962) was the first female associate of the Royal Institute of British Architects (1898) and designed early workers' cottages for Letchworth (1905).

Industrial buildings were encouraged to be 'state of the art' and artistic. Most notable was the

Cecil Hignett's iconic and innovative Spirella corset factory (1912–20), Letchworth Garden City. It represented the Industrial heart of the town in a unique (and paradoxically) industrial adaptation of the Arts and Crafts style, and in the similarly high-quality working conditions and facilities available.

so-called 'Factory of Beauty': the Spirella corset factory (1912–20), designed by Cecil Hignett. This was a major work in the Arts and Crafts style but adapted to a monumental scale for industrial purposes.

Howard had only a limited role in the development of Letchworth, for it was run on more commercial lines than his socialist ideal of common ownership of land, and it did not develop as he had hoped. However, its creation from his theorising, and successful establishment, gave the garden city concept valuable credibility worldwide as a realistic approach to town planning. He lived at Letchworth from 1905 to 1920 when he moved on to his next garden city.

An idealised interior, designed by Barry Parker for his brother Stanley, in Letchworth Garden City, 102 Wilbury Road. Arts and Crafts and historicist styles were strong themes, as epitomised in Parker and Unwin's Letchworth offices.

Seventeen years lapsed before the second garden city (the final true example in England) was founded. In 1919 Howard, then nearly seventy, identified a suitable rural site for a garden city including much of the Panshanger estate near Welwyn, Hertfordshire, 15 miles south of Letchworth down the A1. Some 2,400 acres was acquired and Welwyn Garden City Ltd was floated in April 1920. Howard was more closely involved than at Letchworth. He is even said to have planted an apple tree in the garden of each original house.

For the second garden city, lessons in planning were learnt from the pioneers who designed and inhabited Letchworth. A sensitive master plan

The layout of Welwyn Garden City was masterminded by Louis de Soissons with Howard closely involved (1920). The great axis, formal centre and zoning including informal neighbourhoods were similar to Letchworth.

was provided by Louis de Soissons, a French Canadian architect trained at the Royal Academy and École des Beaux-Arts in Paris. Although the site was quartered by railways, a grand focal Beaux-Arts layout was planned around two formal axes. The main one was Parkway, the imposing civic equivalent to Letchworth's Broadway and The Square, running north to

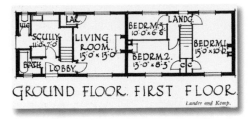

GROUND FLOOR. FIRST FLOOR.

1920s plan for a pair of model semi-detached cottages, Welwyn Garden City.

south alongside the Great Northern Railway. Howardsgate was a cross axis, on an equally imposing scale, leading to the station. The scenic Parkway terminated at the north end in an exedra, The Campus, a semi-circular public space to be surrounded by civic buildings, whose shape reflected the branch line against which it fitted. Functional land-use zoning separated the industry, placed beyond the main north–south railway line. The preferred architectural style moved from the Arts and Crafts rural idyll to a genteel urban Neo-Georgian style, often designed by de Soissons' practice. Like Letchworth, extensive landscaping, based around the spinal, mile-long Parkway axis, was key to the experience and lifestyle of residents and visitors alike.

Growth of Welwyn Garden City was initially slow but by 1926 there were over 1,800 houses and by 1938 a population of 13,500. The population grew in response to success in attracting industry such as the Shredded Wheat factory, Murphy Radio and Roche Products, through which Howard intended to provide economic self-sufficiency. As with Letchworth, industry was housed in its own zone, each factory with a spacious plot, good transport links, and often iconic modern architecture with model conditions for workers. Inevitably Welwyn Garden City was never quite as influential as Letchworth, but it still attracted much interest and many visitors, largely for its layout and architecture rather than as a pioneering social reform project.

The preferred style for Welwyn Garden City houses after the First World War moved from the pre-war Arts and Crafts style of Letchworth to a genteel urban Neo-Georgian style.

The Times in 1948 reported that as a planned settlement, 'Welwyn, though far from perfect, made The New Towns Act possible.'

An entirely different, urgent purpose drove the establishment of the third, and only Scottish, garden city, during the First World War. Rosyth Garden City on the Firth of Forth, near Dunfermline, was built to serve the Admiralty's workmen and their families in the recently established Royal Navy dockyard which opened in 1915. During the six-year period from 1915, 3,000 houses were to be built to replace the shanty town (in

part known as Tin Town) that was rapidly springing up. From 1910 the Edinburgh branch of the Garden Cities Association promoted the garden city concept with the Admiralty, which in 1913 appointed Unwin to prepare a plan. In the event only 1,900 or so houses were built, between 1915 and 1919.

Most buildings at Rosyth were designed or overseen by A. H. Mottram (1886–1953), one of Parker and Unwin's former assistant architects on Hampstead Garden Suburb. Mottram had recently left the Housing Reform

Welwyn Garden City civic centre. Ornamental boulevards linked the buildings. The iconic exedra designed by Louis de Soissons terminated the axial Parkway.

Company Ltd in Cardiff, where he was working on housing schemes including Rhiwbina Garden Suburb (see pp.58–9), to become architect to the Scottish National Housing Company Ltd. During the First World War he designed 1,400 houses for Rosyth Garden City within Unwin's layout, and after the War he supervised its further development. The project stalled in 1925 when the dockyard largely closed, but it was reopened in the Second World War and again became an important naval base.

Rosyth's layout and houses echoed the precedents set in England and adopted in Glasgow Garden Suburb in 1912, reflecting principles established at Bournville, and promoted by Parker and Unwin. Picturesque cottage-style

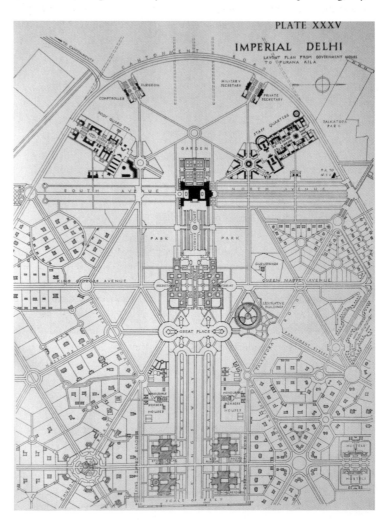

The design of Edwin Lutyens' New Delhi (1912), the British Empire's new state capital. Garden city concepts combined with the Beaux-Arts formality of sweeping vistas and roads. It was the architect's masterpiece, from which he made his name in the 1920s.

houses were arranged at low density and to avoid uniformity, in terraces of four and eight, and semi-detached pairs. Front gardens were hedged with privet, holly and beech, and fenced, linked by broad, tree-lined streets. Generous rear gardens were supplemented by communal green space including a wide greenbelt around the town.

Importantly, Rosyth fulfilled Howard's communal self-sufficiency criterion for a true garden city. To sustain the wider needs of those living in the new houses it had the key employment and commerce, supplemented by municipal, social, educational and religious provision.

Other countries often looked to Britain, as a pioneer industrial society, for a viable community planning precedent. Abroad, garden city principles were taken up enthusiastically, both in the English-speaking world, including the United States, and beyond, particularly in mainland Europe and South America. These principles became the main town planning export of Britain in the twentieth century.

In Germany there was especial interest. Hellerau was the first garden city in the country, founded on the outskirts of Dresden in 1908 by furniture manufacturer Karl Schmidt. The master plan for Falkenburg (Berlin) was prepared by the young architect Bruno Taut in 1913–14. German interest persisted after the First World War. Two key estates in the 1920s used the clean lines of the International (Modern Movement) style: at Dessau (including Gropius's Bauhaus arts and crafts school), and at Weissenhof in Stuttgart, an exhibition site planned by Mies van der Rohe with contributions by Le Corbusier amongst other notable architects.

Two new state capitals for the British Empire were even designed along these lines. In 1912 Canberra (Australia) and New Delhi (India) began to be planned. Canberra's winning plan by Walter Burley Griffin of Chicago was also influenced by the American City Beautiful movement but took many decades to be implemented. It included long vistas, diagonal avenues and star-shaped constellations of roads linking settlements of very low densities of housing, to the point where it hardly felt like a single city. This plan apparently influenced New Delhi, designated the new capital of the Raj in 1911 as a symbol of British power and supremacy. The layout was designed by a planning commission including eminent architects Sir Herbert Baker and Edwin Lutyens and was executed much more rapidly than Canberra. Although numerous historical monuments were retained and indigenous architectural elements were included, Lutyens' Imperial architectural statements dominated, largely constructed in the 1920s (presaged in his 1906 Central Square at Hampstead Garden Suburb). With New Delhi he made his name worldwide, to the point where it was dubbed 'Lutyens' Delhi' by the Viceroy in 1931.

GARDEN SUBURBS
AND VILLAGES

GARDEN SUBURBS AND VILLAGES became far more prevalent than the garden cities because they were easier to establish at smaller scale and were more commercially viable for developers, but in their purpose they were the antithesis of Howard's garden city ideal. The character of these attractive and sometimes exclusive suburbs was clearly inspired by the Garden City Movement and the layouts and architecture were influenced directly or indirectly by Parker and Unwin's work: a spacious layout of appealing groups of houses and gardens, set in attractive roads with open space and amenities, adapting existing landscape features where possible, rather than imposing an entirely man-made character. However, suburbs by definition opposed Howard's model because, instead of new economically self-sufficient towns in green fields with integral employment, they were largely dormitory settlements, attached to existing towns and cities, enlarging the development sprawl that was anathema to staunch adherents to the Movement. Even where these settlements emulated a village in a detached rural location, their small scale meant that they could never be economically self-sufficient as a full-scale town or city would be. Unwin was more pragmatic in this respect than Howard and early on embraced the garden suburb as a more realistic solution than the garden city, designing or advising on many before the First World War.

An attractive, health-giving and useful landscape remained integral to the purpose and character of garden suburbs, as it was to the garden cities. The spaces, both private and public, formed an integrated matrix with the buildings. The key was the enhancement of the buildings with their own gardens, street trees and a variety of communal open spaces reminiscent of Bedford Park, Port Sunlight and Bournville. Large gardens and integral allotment gardens allowed residents to grow their own food, improving their ability to pay rent. Many suburbs enjoyed sporting facilities such as tennis courts, bowling greens and playing fields. The landscape in all its variety was as important to the concept as the buildings and the two were indivisible.

Of the twenty or so garden suburbs founded between 1901 and 1914, the most famous, and prestigious, was Henrietta Barnett's Hampstead

Opposite:
Waterlow Court
(M. H. Baillie Scott,
1909) was an
innovative
Oxbridge-style
quadrangle of flats
for single ladies
in Hampstead
Garden Suburb.

Of twenty or so garden suburbs founded between 1901 and 1914, the most famous, and prestigious, was Henrietta Barnett's Hampstead Garden Suburb. It was founded in 1905 and laid out by Unwin incorporating many existing natural features and trees.

Garden Suburb, founded in 1905. From the first it was conceived as a largely middle-class dormitory. Unwin designed the layout, taking into account the natural features, retaining significant areas of woodland, ancient hedgerows and mature oaks. Lutyens added prestige as the fashionable architectural heavyweight. His major contribution was Central Square: a grand but rather soulless, uninviting civic space at the centre of the suburb, heralding his Imperial civic grandeur at New Delhi. Unwin's integral concept envisaged a natural 'villagey' central gathering point, for all classes, with local amenities based on a range of shops next to a green. Lutyens ignored this. Instead he framed the space on the high point of the suburb with two imposing churches and an educational institute, around a public square. The shops were inconveniently banished to beyond the periphery of the suburb, leaving another unresolved hole in the heart of the community, much as at Letchworth. Strikingly the Suburb's boundary against Hampstead Heath was marked by Unwin's extraordinary concept of a Great Wall (reminiscent

of central European medieval fortified town walls such as Rothenburg). It was designed by Charles Paget Wade and constructed in 1910–12. The Arts and Crafts-style 'look-out towers', with their fine tiling and brickwork, were actually gazebos for the large houses of Linnell Drive whose gardens backed onto the Heath and enjoyed magnificent views of London.

Architecturally, Hampstead Garden Suburb achieved a more consistent quality than Letchworth, even when it was extended after the First World War. The pleasing mix of styles ranged from vernacular in variety, to Lutyens-influenced Queen Anne and Neo-Georgian of the sort used at Bedford Park, to 1930s Modern Movement houses designed by Crickmer (Howard Walk,

Lutyens' St Jude's Church frames the large open space, pairing the equally impressive Free Church. Both dominate views from surrounding streets.

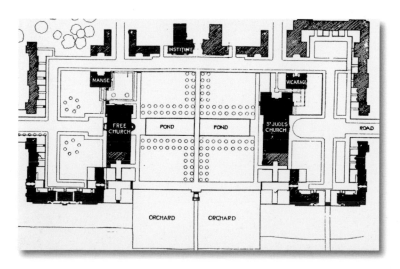

At the heart of Hampstead Garden Suburb, Unwin's proposed bustling and practical communal shops were rejected. Instead shops were banished inconveniently to the edges, replaced by the more prestigious architect Edwin Lutyens' soulless but impressive open space framed by two huge churches and an educational institution.

51

A line of gazebos was designed to look like 'look-out towers' for the large houses of Linnell Drive, Hampstead Garden Suburb. They were set into Charles Paget Wade's Great Wall (1910–12) with spectacular views of Hampstead Heath and distant London.

Lutyens' Free Church, opposite St Jude's Anglican Church.

1935) in the white rendered style sold as 'sun-trap'. It attracted the most prestigious designers of the day, particularly Arts and Crafts architects. Baillie Scott's innovative Waterlow Court (1909) was an Oxbridge-style quadrangle of flats for single ladies; Parker and Unwin's The Orchard (1909) was another quadrangle of small flats, designed for elderly residents for reasonable rents, contrasting with the scale of Guy Dawber's Cotswold-style manor house (1906–8) in Linnell Drive.

In many ways Barnett's suburb followed Howard's key principles: providing decent low-density accommodation in attractive landscaped, spacious surroundings, lived in by a mix of social classes (the expensive houses helped to finance the artisans' accommodation). Its main 'fault' in Howard's terms was in being attached to an existing metropolis, London, rather than a self-sufficient new settlement. It would always be a dormitory suburb, connected to the Metropolis by the Underground from Golders Green station. The high-quality buildings and their leafy setting soon ensured that the residents were mainly from wealthier classes, even in Unwin's renowned Artisans' Quarter (1907–9), rather defeating social reformer Barnett's wish to ensure a cross section of classes (even so the working-classes were confined to a separate quarter). Although Barnett was the (rather patrician) driving force, the suburb was not controlled by a single interest or family, as the industrial villages had been, and buildings were financed through Howard's favoured co-partnerships as well as other models of development.

Brentham Garden Suburb, Ealing, predated Hampstead. It was founded by the great promoter of the co-partnership movement, Henry Vivian,

A lively Hampstead Garden Suburb elevation by the renowned architect M. H. Baillie Scott (1909–10). It is angled across the corner of the junction of Hampstead Way and Meadway, as Unwin would have approved.

53

Sutliffe's design for a typical row of cottages, Brentham Garden Suburb (1911). They rounded a bend in North Way in an organic fashion. Most such drawings for Brentham survive as an extraordinary record of its development.

and was the first development financed in this way. Developed in three main stages, the 60-acre suburb was begun in 1901 with the first co-partnership housing scheme, which became a model for similar schemes for the next two decades. It was an exercise in social engineering – a whole self-contained way of life. In the first stage the houses were to conventional patterns in a tight layout, but the second stage, begun in 1907, had a different character. Its spacious garden suburb plan by Parker and Unwin was typical of their work: leafy, with winding roads, keeping mature trees, and bounded by the River Brent on one side. The housing density was restricted to eight per acre, mainly in rows of pairs and short terraces enclosing allotments and open spaces to the rear.

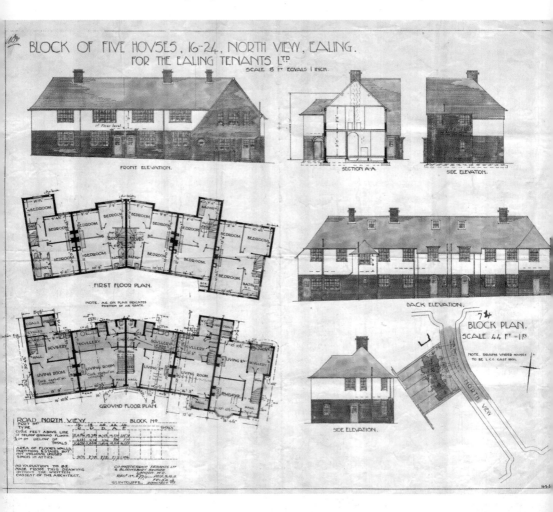

The Brentham
Institute: a
residents' social
and sports club,
c. 1910, by G. L.
Sutcliffe. Designed
in quirky
Germanic style,
It lay at the heart
of the suburb.

At Brentham, the planners and architects achieved striking but harmonious effects on a human scale with a cohesive community. People enjoyed living in their community and its pleasant environs. Houses were mostly in Arts and Crafts style, echoing Bournville with similar materials including half-timbering, decorative brickwork and roughcast rendering. The houses in this second stage, 1907–11, were designed by the young

A typical street
scene of a newly
laid out garden
suburb, at
Brentham, Ealing.
Street trees were
planted alongside
the pavements.

and exuberant architect F. C. Pearson, who was also the architect/planner for Sutton Garden Suburb, Surrey (1912). The buildings were arranged in inviting groups with a rich variety of styles, stepped forward at the ends of terraces to enclose groups and to break up any hint of a monotonous, uniform street frontage. Pearson's two striking 'butterfly plan' blocks of houses terminated views at one junction, set obliquely on their angled plots in true Parker and Unwin manner. Elsewhere huge gables swept down, dominating a detached house frontage or the centre of a row. Greenery abounded in the public and private spaces. Gardens were regarded as 'essential to the happy life of these co-partnership tenants.' They were enclosed by clipped privet hedges, rather than oppressive fences or walls, and contained small flowering trees, and the streets were lined with grass verges planted with many trees, predominantly lime, silver birch and plane. The houses enclosed small, intimate allotment groups.

Surprisingly, at Brentham there was no ornamental park, only a small 'green' in front of the imposing Institute building, which was a social and sports club for the residents. Instead, five acres of 'additional gardens' in seven plots were enclosed by back gardens, mainly used as allotments but also as grassy spaces, and reached by narrow privet-hedged paths through brick archways linking the rows of houses. The attention to detail was remarkable.

Pearson's 1912 design for Sutton Garden Suburb had many features established by Unwin, but only a small proportion was built. The integral communal spaces enclosed by houses are now threatened by development in many such suburbs.

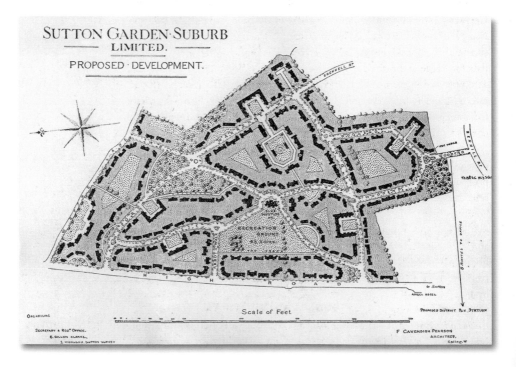

SUTTON GARDEN·SUBURB
LIMITED.
PROPOSED · DEVELOPMENT.

Scale of Feet

F CAVENDISH PEARSON
ARCHITECT,
Ealing. W

Some garden suburbs included housing for single people. G. L. Sutcliffe's Holyoake House, Brentham (c. 1914) had twenty-four flats for single people and retired couples, but did not have a communal kitchen or dining room in the co-operative manner that Unwin thought would encourage a community spirit.

A 12-acre sports field wrapped around the Institute on the northern edge by the River Brent and beyond, the Western Avenue (A40).

For the third stage from 1911, the more mature G. L. Sutcliffe was employed, the architect for Vivian's Co-partnership Tenants Ltd. His housing included more restrained cottages, but his imagination also resulted in the Germanic-style Institute building (1910) with a focal tower, as the suburb's visual and communal focus. At higher density, his quirky 1912 Holyoake House surrounded three sides of a quadrangle facing the road, containing twenty-four flats for single and retired people, on similar lines to Waterlow Court and The Orchard in Hampstead. Despite all the attention to external detail, internally the houses were only supplied with gas and there was no electricity for some time. By 1916 Brentham contained 650 houses and was largely complete. Until the coming of the car it was a largely self-contained community.

Other significant pre-war co-partnership-funded garden suburb developments included Moor Pool, Harborne, Birmingham (built 1907–12) promoted by the industrialist J. S. Nettlefold of GKN. Frederick Martin's sensitive layout and architecture responded to the informality of the valley contours based around a serpentine spinal road running down the bottom of the valley. A range of community facilities promoted healthy minds and bodies, including social and sports clubs, and a central hall, reading room, library, row of shops, village green, bowling green, tennis courts and pond (the Pool). Like Hampstead, the roads were narrower, at 16 feet, than the by-laws stipulated, regarded in this case as sufficient for the neighbourhood traffic while allowing for front gardens, grass verges and street trees essential to the character of the suburb. As far as possible, mature trees were kept. Like Brentham, considerable spaces were enclosed by the back gardens, reached from the streets by narrow hedged paths, in this case for several sets of allotments and a bowling green.

Garden suburbs mushroomed but at differing scales. Humberstone, Leicester, was developed from 1906 by the Anchor Boot & Shoe Co-operative as a co-partnership development with Anchor Tenants. This was the only example where a UK workers' co-operative created a housing co-operative and built a housing estate for members. Burnage Garden Village was built by Manchester Tenants' Association between 1906 and 1911. Its 138 houses in Arts and Crafts style were centred on a bowling green and tennis courts enclosed by houses. Oldham Garden Suburb Movement was founded in 1907, its prime movers being two women of similar stamp to Henrietta Barnett, Mary Higgs and Sarah Lees. Higgs' main work was with the National Association for Women's Lodging Houses, for destitute and vagrant women, and in 1902 she founded the Beautiful Oldham Society to create gardens and improve open spaces in deprived areas of the city. At Fallings Park, Wolverhampton (1908) a model housing exhibition was held but only fifty houses were eventually built.

Liverpool (later Wavertree) Garden Suburb (1910–15), with a density of

Glasgow (now Westerton) Garden Suburb, Bearsden, was built for a housing society formed in 1912 and supervised by Unwin.

eleven houses per acre (rather than the conventional forty-five houses per acre in inner-city Liverpool) was another pioneer city suburb, and its development was widely reported. The first phase was designed by Unwin, with houses in the second phase of development by G. L. Sutcliffe. Here again efforts were made to include existing features such as trees and meandering road lines. Recreational facilities included tennis courts, bowling greens and an Institute. Eventually 360 houses were built.

In Wales the Garden City Movement made a considerable mark from 1910 in Glamorgan, around Cardiff and Swansea, responding to slum clearance, and the need for improved miners' housing in the Valleys. Perhaps the most outstanding example in Wales was Rhiwbina Garden Village, Glamorgan, founded in 1912 with the first houses completed in 1913. It was laid out for the Housing Reform Company Ltd in Cardiff to a master plan by Unwin. Unwin was involved elsewhere in the area, in 1910 with the layout for a Cottage Exhibition for Swansea Corporation, and, from 1915, with the garden suburb at Barry, whose architect was T. Alwyn Lloyd.

In Scotland the first garden suburb was the Glasgow (now Westerton) Garden Suburb, Bearsden. A housing society was formed in 1912 to create co-operatively-owned housing communities for the working classes at affordable prices. Only 81 of 120 planned houses were constructed by the First World War – which stopped development – but further development occurred in the 1930s and 1940s. The first houses were designed by J. A. W. Grant with supervision by Unwin. Architecturally the Arts and Crafts

Silver End, Essex (1926) for F. H. Crittall's metal window factory was a late industrialist's village but employed the most up-to-date Modern Movement style.

Previous pages:
The extensive
Whiteley Village
was built from
1914 as a
retirement village
for people of
slender means but
good character.
It followed
the almshouse
tradition, using
a £1m bequest
by the murdered
department
store owner
William Whiteley.

influence included sweeping roof lines, timber-framed gables, and slate-roofed and harled cottages, united visually by the repetition of these features and the consistent use of privet hedges of regulation height. Many trees lined the streets as part of the original concept, with trees and shrubs donated by Sir John Stirling Maxwell, a local founder of the Tenants' Society.

Competitive exhibitions to demonstrate economical and innovative methods continued to be important, following the example of the 1905 Letchworth £150 houses competition. Gidea Park, Romford, begun by developers in 1910, held a '100 Best Houses' exhibition in 1911 in which cottages and houses were designed by more than a hundred architects, many of considerable reputation including Parker and Unwin, Baillie Scott, T. Gordon Jackson, Philip Tilden, and Clough Williams-Ellis. By the following year 140 houses had been built. The competition was restricted to 'small houses' of four bedrooms, for £500, and 3-bedroom 'cottages', for £375. Convenient and labour-saving plans were encouraged. Many of the usually detached houses were in Tudor styles, roughcast, colour-washed, or sometimes half-timbered and of high quality materials. Landscaping was important and the plots were 'of good size' to match the generous proportions of the houses.

Industrialists' villages with garden suburb characteristics were still created occasionally. Sir James Reckitt's Hull Garden Village (1907) followed low-density principles, but its cosy traditional architecture contrasted sharply with Silver End village, Essex (1926), built for the metal window manufacturer F. H. Crittall and Co., in pioneering Modern Movement style. Silver End is a startling monument to Crittall's products as well as a rare, extensive display of sleek architectural lines. Along with the rows of terraces and semi-detached houses, three substantial detached houses were imaginatively designed for managers, each unique and prominent from the main road. Only a fragment of the village was built, as the Depression and the Second World War halted further development. The large size of the village hall, hotel and former department store were evidence of original intentions.

Whiteley Village was a unique self-contained retirement village. The site was bought in 1911 and the buildings constructed from 1914 using a £1m bequest by William Whiteley, the murdered philanthropist and owner of the London department store Whiteley's. Set deep in Surrey woodland, near Cobham, it was planned in eight segments around an octagonal village centre with a monumental centrepiece. It was built to the highest quality with designs by seven of the most prestigious Arts and Crafts architects of the day including Reginald Blomfield, Aston Webb and Ernest Newton. As a pioneering community, self-sufficient in its facilities for retired persons, it housed all classes as long as they were of good character and sound mind, unaffected by any infectious diseases, nor convicted of any criminal

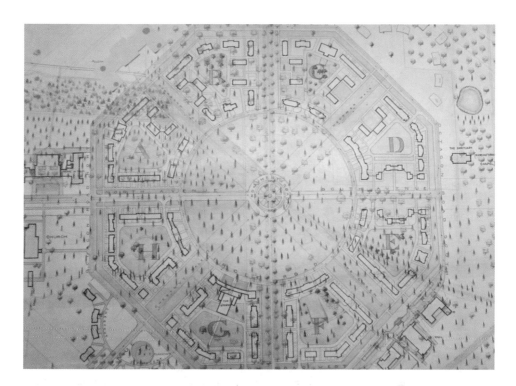

offence. More than 260 cottages housed over 300 people. Although rooted in the more modest almshouse tradition, the scale, design, quality and architectural ambition of Whiteley's vision made it outstanding and unparalleled as a self-contained community until decades later.

Abroad, garden suburbs were embraced with enthusiasm. In the British Colonies notable suburbs included, in Australia, Haberfield (Sydney, founded in 1901, apparently independently from Howard's theories), and Colonel Light Gardens (Mitcham, Adelaide, planned from 1917). In South Africa, Pinelands, Cape Town, was designed in 1920 by A. J. Thompson, who had recently planned Swanpool Garden Suburb, Lincoln (see below). The renowned landscape designer Thomas Mawson (1861–1933) planned several suburbs in Canada between 1910 and 1914 including in Ottawa, Victoria, Calgary, and Regina, although these were only partially implemented or remained unexecuted, largely for reasons of expense in recently founded cities. In *Civic Art* (1911), Thomas Mawson discussed the principles of town planning, for the first time integrating landscape architecture as a distinct and important aspect.

After the Great War the principles of the Garden City Movement gained influence in government circles, particularly with the pressing need for

The striking layout at Whiteley Village is unique and formal, with the rows of cottages framing many open vistas and spaces, and fine buildings around an imposing central monument to its founder.

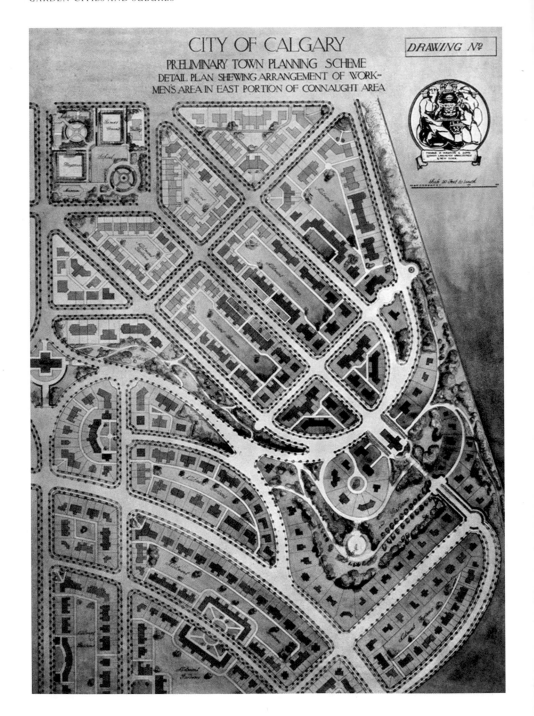

'Homes Fit For Heroes' and with Unwin established as a government adviser. At its heart was Howard's creation during the 1920s of the second garden city at Welwyn. Notable post-war garden suburbs included Swanpool Garden Suburb, Lincoln (1919), designed by Thompson, but the 113 houses built in Arts and Crafts style were only a fragment of the planned 2,000–3,000 houses. More extensively, architect Herbert Collins (1885–1975), also a friend of Unwin, had a great influence on the development of Southampton's suburbs. He too was involved with the development of Welwyn Garden City and was both a disciple of Howard and an advocate of garden suburbs. He proposed a garden city outside Southampton, on which Howard advised personally. Collins' designs in Southampton were regarded as some of the finest housing estates in the southern counties, particularly the Orchards Way and Uplands Estates.

Westfield War Memorial Village, Lancaster (1919), commemorated soldiers' lives lost in the First World War. It was a rural working village with workshops for men disabled in the war, and for able-bodied men, without any hint of charity. The brainchild of Lancastrian Thomas Mawson, based on ideas he had set out in his book *An Imperial Obligation: Industrial Villages for Partially Disabled Service Men* (1917), it was financed by Herbert Storey and built on his country house estate. Stone and roughcast cottages with Westmorland slate roofs and open frontages overlooked tree-lined streets, and the estate was entered via a pair of imposing gates. A bowling green reflected Mawson's enthusiasm for the benefits of fresh air and exercise. The centrepiece was a war memorial based on a fine, bronze statue by Jennifer Delahunt of a battlefield scene: a soldier giving his wounded comrade-in-arms a drink from his canteen.

Spurred on by the effects of the Tudor Walters Report (1918) on legislation and municipal housing guidance, and influenced by the Garden City Movement, local authorities after the First World War developed extensive suburbs and housing estates, superseding the need for co-partnerships. The most notable of these included Becontree (1921) and Watling Estate (1926) by London County Council, Perry Bar in Birmingham (1928), the Priory Estate, Dudley (1929), and Speke Estate, Liverpool (1936), planned by Sir Lancelot Keay. Manchester City Council's Wythenshawe (1931), with which Barry Parker was closely associated into the 1940s, was regarded by him as the third English garden city.

Opposite: Thomas Mawson's proposed suburb in Calgary, Canada (c. 1910–14) followed garden city principles, using pairs and short terraces of houses lining serpentine roads, culs-de-sac, village greens, and allotments surrounded by houses.

Westfield War Memorial Village, Lancashire (1919), commemorated lives lost in the First World War. Mawson's design combined houses with workshops, surrounding a village green focused on a moving bronze sculpture of two brothers in arms.

The Liberal Catholic Church was the first church in Letchworth Garden City to be built (1923) and consecrated (1924) for an offshoot of the Catholic Church. The west end is timbered in contrast to the other roughcast walls, in an unusual application of the Arts and Crafts style.

The Letchworth community banner was the focus of parades for years, here with Ebenezer Howard in front of it in 1911.

the rest of the country. Temperance was often a key element, suggested by Howard as a 'local option'. In Letchworth The Skittles Inn (Parker and Unwin, 1907) was an 'olde English inn' which offered a traditional skittle alley and bar but no alcohol, as voted for by the residents for many years. Welwyn Garden City was not so strict and allowed The Cherry Tree, a 'wet canteen' occupying a reused army surplus hut made elegant on the outside by trelliswork.

"CORONATION" LETCHWORTH. 1911.

Letchworth, Howgills Friends Meeting House.

Howgills Meeting House, Letchworth Garden City, reflects the style of many houses in Letchworth, as do many Friends' Meeting Houses in other places.

At the heart of the garden suburbs a social and educational institution drew the community together. In Brentham the Institute was a social and sports club for the residents, with similar social and educational buildings elsewhere, including the Club House in Hampstead (Parker and Unwin, 1909), and the Institute in Wavertree, Liverpool. Schools were naturally provided where the settlement was of sufficient size, and adult education

The Mayday procession at Letchworth Garden City (1909), through the modern shopping streets at the heart of the town, revived perceived days of 'merrie olde England'.

MAY REVELS GARDEN CITY 1909 10.

such as that offered by Henrietta Barnett's Institute in Hampstead, was regarded as 'improving' and a valuable alternative to drink. The Cloisters, Letchworth (1906–7) was built as an open-air adult school, an expensive experiment for its donor, Annie Jane Lawrence.

Recreation drew together the community of most garden cities and suburbs. At Letchworth, Howard Park was quickly laid out as the main formal public park, contrasting in style with Norton Common, which was left largely unaltered, but with a broad grassed avenue linking the civic centre with outer areas. Local horticultural societies flourished and encouraged tenants to make the best use of their plots. The Brentham School of Gardening allowed tenants to showcase the variety of shrubs and flowers that would 'flourish best

Divers at The Cloisters, Letchworth: one of various unconventional activities that proliferated in the early days of the pioneering First Garden City.

The Cloisters, Letchworth (1906–7) was an open-air adult school, built as an experiment in an extraordinary style and form for its philanthropic donor, Annie Jane Lawrence.

in the good soil of Ealing' and the Horticultural Society was to assist 'many a resident to whom his unwalled garden has proved a new and delightful world'. At Wavertree, in 1911, 'A bowling green and two lawn tennis courts have been laid, and a gravel playground about half an acre in extent has been provided for the children and furnished with swings and see-saws.' The bowling green and tennis courts were hidden between the houses in Thingwall Road and Nook Rise. Fieldway Green — which had been earmarked as the site of tennis courts — was the scene of Rose Queen Festivals for many years. At Brentham, Ealing, the great Wimbledon champion Fred Perry grew up and learned to play tennis with the other boys on the tennis courts by the Institute.

The powerhouse and economy of the self-contained garden city were based on shopping and work. Shopping was usually catered for in a range of local shops. The garden cities developed central shopping, eventually in several parades. Oddly at Welwyn all the town's citizens were initially required to shop in the same store, The Welwyn Stores. This subsidiary of the Garden City company opened in 1921 and held a monopoly for ten years before further shops were permitted, delaying the development of a main

Access to communal open space was essential for garden city and suburb residents as part of Howard's ethos of the town meeting the country, and to foster community spirit. Shown here is Howard Park and Garden, Letchworth Garden City (1904–11) in which the Mrs Howard Memorial Hall stood.

HOWARD PARK, LETCHWORTH.

Conventional activities included bowls. Most garden suburbs had a bowling green, tennis courts and a recreation ground. Brentham Garden Suburb, c. 1912.

Schools were essential for the families of thriving garden city and suburb communities. At Norton Road School, Letchworth Garden City (c. 1910), the garden was an important element.

shopping centre along Howardsgate for some years. Suburbs usually had a small integral parade of shops conveniently placed, sometimes as part of the community focus (such as Moor Pool, Birmingham, near the central community halls and tennis courts), but the modest Silver End settlement in Essex boasted a department store. Lutyens' grand civic gesture at the heart of Hampstead Garden Suburb, which could have formed a thriving community focus, instead effectively and inconveniently banished shops to the edges of the large community.

The palatial
and stylish
interior of the
Broadway Cinema,
Letchworth
Garden City, 1936.

Picture palaces
were popular. The
Palace Cinema,
Letchworth
Garden City,
re-fronted in
modern style in
the 1930s.

Shops were important both to serve the residents and as part of the local economy. Welwyn Garden City's own department store was in the 1920s the only shop in the town. The much smaller Silver End village in Essex also had a department store. Most suburbs had parades of smaller shops.

Sources of nearby work were essential to the success of garden cities, whether via service industries or manufacturing in one of the integral industrial zones. The progressive industrialist, the American William Kincaid, chose Letchworth in its early days as an ideal place for his Spirella corset factory and to provide model conditions for the workers to live in. He provided facilities rarely found elsewhere, including baths, showers, gymnastics classes, a library, free eye tests and bicycle repairs, and on the top floor the factory even had a magnificent ballroom. The bookbinders Dents were another key employer from early days. Welwyn, the second garden city, became a fully functioning town, with a full range of facilities including industry, and the architecturally notable Shredded Wheat factory (designed by de Soissons, 1925), but because of better travel links with London it became more of a commuter town than Letchworth. By contrast the smaller garden suburbs, by definition attached to conurbations which

An industrial icon of Welwyn Garden City was de Soissons' Modern Movement Shredded Wheat factory (1925), placed close to the railway for transporting goods.

provided work, actively discouraged industry, as their residents serviced the adjacent town or city. The larger suburb settlements, for example the munitions housing schemes and the municipal satellite estates such as Becontree and Wythenshawe, were usually closely linked to industry. Garden villages were usually planned with integral employment.

Today garden cities, suburbs and villages continue to fulfil the hopes of their founders and planners, providing the standard of living and quality of life in their architecture and environs that was initially intended. Many have active residents' associations and strong community spirit and activities. These communities are proud of their history and how they have continued, some for a century and more, to provide a pleasant and attractive place to live, and, in the case of garden cities, employment. This is reflected and promoted in published histories and community

A crested china sofa epitomised the welcome and home comforts to be found in Letchworth Garden City.

Packing boxes in the Shredded Wheat factory, where workers enjoyed higher standards of employment than most people in 1920s Britain.

Girls' rest room, Shredded Wheat Factory, Welwyn Garden City. The workers were unusually well provided for.

websites, which usually include a strong link with their historic origins and an understanding of the purpose of their foundation. These settlements are often highly sought-after by potential residents who recognise the lifestyle benefits and attractive surroundings. Perhaps they are not exactly Utopia, but the improving intentions of the founders and planners have been valued and to a great extent preserved.

FURTHER READING

Many of the garden city and garden suburb websites below have individual detailed histories with further references and electronic resources.

BOOKS

Beevers, R. *The Garden City Utopia: A Critical Biography of Ebenezer Howard*. Macmillan, 1988.

Buder, S. *Visionaries and Planners: The Garden City Movement and the Modern Community*. Oxford University Press, 1990.

Chalkley, L., and Shiach, M. (eds). *Rosyth: Garden City and Royal Dockyard*. Rosyth Garden City Millennium Project, 2005.

Creedon, A. *Only a Woman: Henrietta Barnett — Social Reformer and Founder of Hampstead Garden Suburb*. Phillimore, 2006.

Creese, W. *The Search for the Environment: The Garden City Before and After*. Yale, 1966.

Harrison, M. *Bournville: Model Village to Garden Suburb*. Phillimore, 1999.

Howard, E. *Tomorrow: A Peaceful Path to Real Reform*. Routledge, 2004 (originally published 1898).

Howard, E. *Garden Cities of Tomorrow*. Introduction by F. Osborn. Faber & Faber, 1965 (and later edns [originally published 1902]).

Hubbard, E. and Shippobottom, M. *A Guide to Port Sunlight Village*. Liverpool University Press, 1988.

Kornwolf, J. D. *M. H. Baillie Scott and the Arts and Crafts Movement*. Johns Hopkins Press, 1972.

Mawson, T. *Civic Art Studies in Town Planning, Parks, Boulevards and Open Spaces*. Batsford, 1911.

Meacham, S. *Regaining Paradise: Englishness and the Early Garden City Movement*. Yale, 1999.

Miller, M. *Raymond Unwin: Garden Cities and Town Planning*. Leicester University Press, 1992.

Miller, M. *Letchworth: The First Garden City*. Phillimore, 2002.

Miller, M. *Hampstead Garden Suburb: An Arts and Crafts Utopia?* Phillimore, 2006.

Miller, M. *English Garden Cities: An Introduction*. English Heritage, 2010.

On the eve of the First World War, *Punch* gently ridiculed the eccentrics and ideas associated with garden-city dwellers (1 July 1914).

GARDEN CITY WASHING-DAY.

OUR SENSITIVE ARTIST INSISTS ON A HARMONIOUS COLOUR-SCHEME.

Morris, W. *News from Nowhere: Or an Epoch of Rest* …. Reeves and Turner, 1890 (and many later editions).

Moss-Eccardt, J. *Ebenezer Howard: An Illustrated Life of Sir Ebenezer Howard 1850–1928*. Shire, 1973.

Muthesius, H. (D. Sharp ed.) *The English House*. 3 vols. Frances Lincoln, 2007 (facsimile of 1904 edition).

Reid, A. *Brentham: A History of the Pioneer Garden Suburb*. Brentham Heritage Society, 2001.

Unwin, R. *Town Planning in Practice: An Introduction to the Art of Designing Cities and Suburbs*. T. Fisher Unwin, 1909.

Ward, S.V. *The Garden City: Past, Present, and Future*. Spon, 1992.

Waymark, J. *Thomas Mawson: Life, Gardens and Landscapes*. Frances Lincoln, 2009.

WEBSITES

See Places to Visit, below, for web addresses of individual places.

Letchworth Garden City and garden cities generally:
www.gardencitymuseum.org

Town and Country Planning Association: www.tcpa.org.uk

By the end of the 'War To End All Wars' *Punch* still mocked, but also lauded the residents who were by now a valued part of Britain (3 July 1918).

PLACES TO VISIT

The year of foundation is given in brackets.

UNITED KINGDOM

Bedford Park, West London (1875): www.bedfordpark.org

Bournville, Birmingham (1895): www.bvt.org.uk/about-us/the-bournville-story

Brentham Garden Suburb, Ealing, London (1901): www.brentham.com

Burnage Garden Village, Manchester (1906): www.burnageheritage.org

Hull Garden Village, East Yorkshire (1907): www.gardenvillagehull.co.uk

Hampstead Garden Suburb, London (1907): www.hgs.org.uk/history; www.hgstrust.org/history

BEATING THE U-BOATS IN OUR GARDEN SUBURB.
SATURDAY EVENING ONION PARADE.

Humberstone Garden Village, Leicester (1906):
    www.anchortenants.org/origins/index.html
Jordans Village, Buckinghamshire (1919): www.seergreenandjordans.org.uk
Letchworth Garden City (1903): www.gardencitymuseum.org (includes
    other garden cities)
Moorpool, Harborne, Birmingham (1908):
    www.moorpool.com/moorpool.ra/
New Earswick, York (1902): www.jrht.org.uk/node/26
Port Sunlight, Merseyside (1888): www.portsunlightvillage.com
Rhiwbina Garden Village (1912): www.rhiwbina.co.uk
Rosyth, Dunfermline, Fife (1915): www.s1rosyth.com/memories/a-brief-
    history-of-rosyth.html
Saltaire, Bradford (1851): www.saltaire.yorks.com
Silver End, Essex (1926): www.silverend.org
Sutton Garden Suburb, Sutton, Surrey (1912): www.suttongardensuburb.org
Wavertree Garden Suburb, Liverpool (1910):
    www.walkingbook.co.uk/liverpool/pages/page10.htm;
    http://wavsoc.awardspace.info/wgs/index.html
Welwyn Garden City (1920): http://welwyngarden-heritage.org
Westerton Garden Suburb, Bearsden, Glasgow (1913):
    www.westertonvillage.org.uk
Whiteley Village Museum, Cobham, Surrey (1911) by appointment only.
    Contact Whiteley Village Historical Society via the website:
    www.whiteleyvillage.org.uk/history_section.php

ABROAD
Colonel Light Gardens, Mitcham, Adelaide, South Australia (1915):
    www.clghs.org.au
Dessau, Saxony-Anhalt, Germany (1920s)
Haberfield, Sydney, Australia (1901):
    www.dictionaryofsydney.org/entry/haberfield
Hellerau, Dresden, Germany (1909):
    www.hellerau/org/english/hellerau/history/the-garden-city
Pinelands, Cape Town, South Africa (1919):
    http://gadgeteer.co.za/historyofpinelands
Mount Royal Garden Suburb, Calgary, Canada (1914):
    www.town.mount-royal.qc.ca
Riverside, Chicago, Illinois, USA: http://riverside-
    illinois.com/History.htm
Weissenhof, Stutttgart (1927):
    www.weissenhof2002.de/english/weissenhof.html

INDEX